MW00800264

This book was provided for

Global Gathering
Brazil

by

Bettendorf
Public Library
Foundation

Raising money to support,
enhance and preserve
Bettendorf Public Library
programs and services.

Building Brasilia

Building Brasilia

Photographs by Marcel Gautherot

Kenneth Frampton, with contributions by Sergio Burgi and Samuel Titan, Jr.

Lake Paranoá (northern lake), with the Monumental Axis in the background, *c.* 1960

Contents

The National Congress palace, *c.* 1960

I Photography and Architecture: Marcel Gautherot in Brasilia

Sergio Burgi

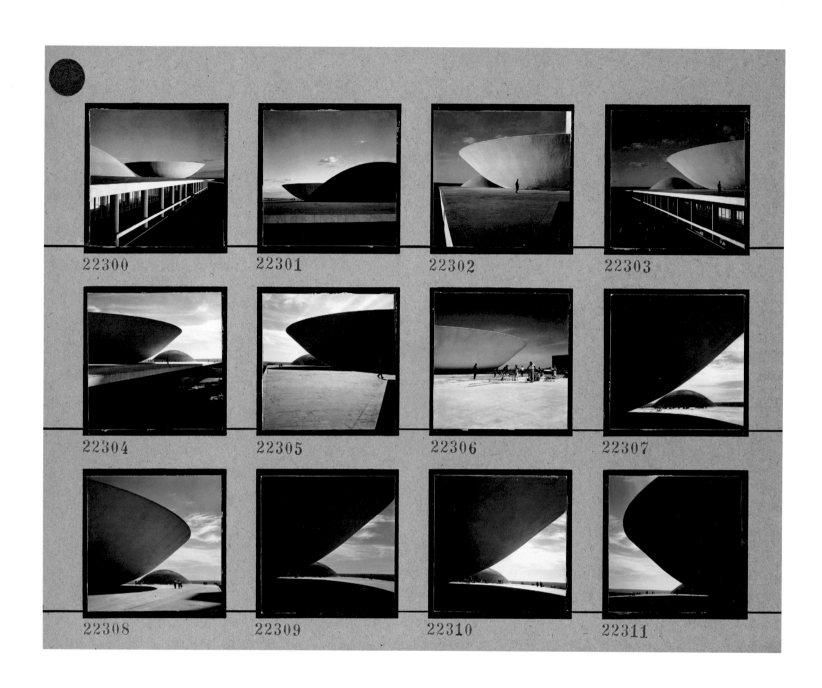

Several views of the National Congress palace on a contact sheet
in the Instituto Moreira Salles' Marcel Gautherot collection, *c.* 1960

This publication is dedicated to the simultaneous celebration of Brasilia's fiftieth anniversary and the centennial of the birth of Marcel Gautherot (1910-1996). By now, the city of Brasilia needs no introduction; this book introduces Gautherot, the French photographer whose extensive body of work is mostly focused on Brazil, and whose images of Brasilia deserve pride of place.

Gautherot's work is of signal importance to the history of Brazilian photography in the twentieth century. On his arrival here in 1939, he focused his lens upon vast tracts of the country and the broadest variety of subjects, always with an exceptional sense of aesthetics, the fruit of constant elaboration of the two basic elements of his background — architecture and ethnographic photography — and, no less, an intense dialogue with central figures of Brazilian culture such as poet Carlos Drummond de Andrade, urban planner Lucio Costa, sociologist Edison Carneiro, landscape artist Roberto Burle Marx and architect Oscar Niemeyer, with whom he cultivated a longstanding friendship and a professional partnership.

It is therefore no accident that Gautherot's sharp, precise gaze has bequeathed us the most complete visual record of modern architecture ever attempted in Brazil, of which his photographs of the building of Brasilia represent the apex. It was at around the age of fifty — as a mature and well-established photographer — that Gautherot produced this comprehensive record of the capital's construction, published here for the first time in a book exclusively dedicated to the subject.[1]

Born in Paris on 14 July 1910, Marcel André Félix Gautherot was the son of a mason and a textile factory worker. In 1925, at the age of fifteen, and already an architect's apprentice, he enrolled in a night course in architecture at the École Nationale des Arts Décoratifs (now the École Nationale Supérieure des Arts Décoratifs, or Ensad).

Although Gautherot did not finish the course, during the five years he spent in college his academic background and practice as an architect and decorator aligned with the emergence of the modern movement in architecture. Among other landmarks, the Esprit Nouveau pavilion designed by Le Corbusier and Pierre Jeanneret for the Parisian Decorative Arts Exhibition of 1925 served the young Gautherot as an example of the rejection of ornamentation and the affirmation of architecture as a pure creation of the spirit based on harmonious form and the primacy of geometry and functionality.

During 1927 and 1928, Gautherot worked at Gustave Moeder's furniture store in Strasbourg, designing furniture for a modern apartment: lacquered and nickel-plated objects that combined sobriety with geometry, befitting his own preference for simplicity and functionalism. In 1927, he visited the Weissenhof Siedlung in Stuttgart, a public exhibition of the modern way of living in a model city that involved the participation of new architects such as Walter Gropius, Mies van der Rohe and Le Corbusier. In 1929, Gautherot joined a group of students who were participating in a contest sponsored by the Austrian furniture company Thonet-Mundus. The jury (which included Pierre Jeanneret, from Le Corbusier's studio, as well as Marcel Breuer, Gropius and Van der Rohe) awarded the group two first and two second prizes. Finally, in 1930, Gautherot participated in the Sohlberg Congress, a conference of liberals, communists and socialists attended by young French and German students concerned with the rise of nationalism

1 The Marcel Gautherot collection, currently housed and preserved at the Instituto Moreira Salles, is comprised of approximately 25,000 images, including negatives, contact sheets, slides and original photographs, as well as books and documents. Brasilia is the subject of some 3,000 of the images, most taken with Rolleiflex and Hasselblad cameras and 6 x 6 cm negatives, while a very few were shot with larger cameras using 10 x 12 cm negatives.

Detail of sculpture adorning the façade of Mitla palace, Oaxaca, Mexico, 1937
General view of the Acropolis, Athens, Greece, 1930s
Fishermen, Mexiana Island, Pará, c. 1943

during the period. The socialist magazine *Notre Temps*—the organ of the 'new European generations'—published a special edition on the congress, in which Gautherot appears on the cover as one of the French speakers. His 'Discours sur l'architecture française'—based on Le Corbusier's writings and Bauhaus ideals—was a clear defence of the *esprit nouveau* and of modern architecture.

Le Corbusier's declaration that 'Architecture is the masterly, correct and magnificent play of masses brought together in light',[2] as well as his sense of 'light as the foundation of architecture' evidently made a powerful impression on Gautherot in his formative years as an architect, as did his new interest in photography, given that light was explicitly regarded as the shaping element of formal and aesthetic decisions in architecture as well as photography. This idea runs through Gautherot's work from the mid-1930s, when he began to devote himself primarily to photography, to the period that extended from 1940 to 1960, when he established his work as a photographer of architecture in Brazil. In his new homeland, he declared that 'photography *is* architecture',[3] and that anyone who did not understand architecture would never be able to take a good photograph. (It is incidentally worth remembering Le Corbusier's great trip through South America in 1929, during which he delivered lectures in Buenos Aires and later travelled to São Paulo and to Rio de Janeiro, a city for which he created iconoclastic urban planning projects: his participation in 1936 as project consultant for the Ministry of Education and Health building in Rio, a landmark of modern Brazilian architecture, which Gautherot photographed to beautiful effect, was a consequence of this trip.)

During the 1930s, Gautherot's interest in photography led him to Alliance Photo in Paris, the first French-based international photo agency, at which other names were beginning to stand out: René Zuber, Emeric Feher, Pierre Boucher and Pierre Verger. In around 1934, he shot a photo series in Greece. In 1935, he took part in the 'Affiche-Photo-Typo' exhibition, which included photographers from Alliance Photo and designers such as Le Houerf and Robert Pontabry. A year later, in 1936, Gautherot began to collaborate with the Musée de l'Homme in the Palais de Chaillot, in Paris. In 1937, he and Pontabry designed the museum's new screening room, and, in partnership with Pierre Verger, Gautherot dedicated himself to organizing and photographing the ethnographic collection.

In a later interview, Gautherot declared that 'above all, photography was a result of my desire to travel'.[4] In fact, late in 1936, at the service of the Musée de l'Homme, he undertook a trip to Mexico that lasted several months. He remained there until the beginning of 1937 to photograph the country's various regions and cultures. During his stay, he met Manuel Álvarez Bravo and Álvarez Bravo's wife Lola. Later, Gautherot said that Cartier-Bresson and Álvarez Bravo were his 'model photographers'.

In 1939, once again on assignment for the Musée de l'Homme, Gautherot travelled to Brazil, instigated by his reading of Jorge Amado's novel *Jubiabá*, which had been published in France in 1938. Curiously, instead of going to Bahia, where the novel is set, his original plan had been to travel through the Brazilian Amazon and later to explore the Peruvian Andes, photographing nature and the populations of those regions.[5] However, with the outbreak of the Second World War, the photographer was drafted into the French Army in Dakar, Senegal.

2 LE CORBUSIER. *Vers une architecture*. Paris: Crès, 1923.

3 ANGOTTI-SALGUEIRO, Heliana. 'Fotografando a arquitetura: barroca, vernacular e moderna'. *In O olho fotográfico: Marcel Gautherot e seu tempo*. São Paulo: Faap, 2007, p. 253.

4 Interview with Lygia Segala, 07.12.1989. SEGALA, Lygia. 'Bumba-meu-boi Brasil'. *In*: GAUTHEROT, Marcel. *O Brasil de Marcel Gautherot*. São Paulo: Instituto Moreira Salles, 2001.

5 Marcel Gautherot returned to the Amazon on several occasions. Some of the photographs he took have been reproduced in *Norte*, edited by Milton Hatoum and Samuel Titan, Jr. (São Paulo: Instituto Moreira Salles, 2009).

Palafitas near Manaus, Amazonas, *c.* 1944
Ministry of Education and Health, Rio de Janeiro, *c.* 1946

Senhor Bom Jesus de Matosinhos Church, Congonhas do Campo, Minas Gerais, *c.* 1942
Sculptures of the prophets Jeremiah, Ezekiel and Joel by Aleijadinho in Congonhas do Campo, Minas Gerais, *c.* 1942

Rapidly demobilized after the 1940 armistice, Gautherot chose not to return to occupied Paris, where the activities of the Musée de l'Homme had been interrupted. Instead, he decided to go back to Brazil and, ultimately, to establish himself there as a photographer.

In Rio de Janeiro (then the capital of Brazil), Gautherot quickly made friends and engaged in dialogue with a circle of artists and intellectuals who were soon to become outstanding figures in Brazilian culture. At the headquarters of the Serviço do Patrimônio Histórico e Artístico Nacional (Sphan) [National Historic and Artistic Heritage Service], founded in 1937 and housed in the Ministry of Education and Health building, Gautherot met the scholar (and institution's director) Rodrigo Melo Franco de Andrade, who invited the expatriate to work on his projects for documenting cultural heritage, particularly that of the colonial period. The Sphan's projects were oriented by the attempt to construct a national identity, especially during the period in which Gustavo Capanema headed the Ministry of Education and Public Health. Capanema underscored the importance of the link between the preservation of Brazil's colonial heritage (and of the baroque style as expressed in the art and architecture of Minas Gerais) and the modern architecture being produced in Brazil.

Thus, from 1940 onwards, Gautherot found himself involved in the Sphan's documentary efforts, particularly with regard to the baroque architecture of Minas Gerais and the work of the sculptor Aleijadinho in Congonhas do Campo.[6] Simultaneously, very much in the spirit of Lucio Costa and Gustavo Capanema, Gautherot added another, vigorously modern focus to the historical one. Here his photographs of Burle Marx's work

in progress stand out—particularly the latter's projects for Rio's mountain range and, later, for Rio's Flamengo landfill—as do those of Niemeyer's work, beginning with the Pampulha complex in Belo Horizonte and culminating in the photographs of the construction of Brasilia during the latter half of the 1950s.

From 1958 until the inauguration of Brasilia, on 21 April 1960, Gautherot assiduously frequented, at Niemeyer's invitation, the new capital's enormous construction site, returning to the city on other occasions until the 1970s. The result is a collection of three thousand images, many of which were widely disseminated in official Brazilian government publications and in architectural magazines the world over. These photographs represent the apex of Gautherot's work and, undoubtedly, one of the high points of twentieth-century photography of architecture.

From the beginning, the new capital proved to be a challenge and an unprecedented opportunity for Gautherot's sense that there was a fundamental unity between architecture and photography. Where else but in Brasilia could he have conducted a fuller demonstration of this idea? A preliminary glimpse of the final result may be seen in the shot of the National Congress at sunrise. In this, as in other images from the series to which it belongs, there is nothing fortuitous about the positioning of the camera; it evinces a vocation for abstraction and pre-visualization of the image governed by a desire to capture the structural design of the architectural grouping. In turn, this is only fully evinced thanks to Gautherot's twofold ability to wait for the best and brightest light and his precise control of film exposure, a combination that ensured a high definition of infinite gradations of light in its interaction with

6 A selection of this material may be seen in *Paisagem moral* (São Paulo: Instituto Moreira Salles, 2009).

constructed surfaces—designing, covering, or reflecting all the nuances of volume, plane and texture in construction.

In Brasilia, all the elements of Gautherot's aesthetic background and photographic gaze converged. In the city of Lucio Costa and Oscar Niemeyer, elements of Brazil's architectural past and natural landscapes were submitted to a new, highly modern synthesis that captured the imagination of a photographer who was always interested, as much because of his early education as because of his unique biography, in each one of these constituent elements—landscape, heritage, aesthetic modernity and social renewal.

The National Congress palace, *c.* 1960

The Ministerial Esplanade and the National Congress palace under construction, *c.* 1958

II Construct and Construction: Brasilia's Development

Kenneth Frampton

'We were only saddened by the conviction that it would be unfeasible to ensure the workers the standard of living assigned them by the Pilot Plan, which situated them, as would have been only fair, within the collective housing areas so as to allow their children to grow up with the other children of Brasilia in a friendly, impartial association designed to eliminate frustration and fit them for the new station that would be theirs when in time the just claims of humanity were fully granted. We realized to our regret that the social conditions in force conflicted at this point with the spirit of the Pilot Plan, creating problems it was impossible to solve on the drawing board and even demanding—as some of the more ingenuous suggested— a social architecture that would lead us nowhere without a socialist basis. Once again, it was brought home to us that all we could do was to support the progressive movements that envisage a better and a happier world.'

OSCAR NIEMEYER, *Módulo* magazine, n. 18, 1960

The Catetinho, provisional housing built entirely out of wood for President Juscelino Kubitschek during the construction of Brasilia, *c.* 1958

Alvorada

Brasilia was inaugurated at a particularly susceptible moment in the political and cultural modernization of the country, when within a decade legislation was passed that facilitated land expropriation as a planning tool with which to respond to the large-scale rural migration into the cities. At the same time certain significant developments took place in the fields of architecture and art; above all, of course, the emergence of a specifically Brazilian language in these areas, originating in the late 1930s in the pioneering work of such figures as Oscar Niemeyer, Affonso Reidy, Cândido Portinari and Roberto Burle Marx. Taking this work as his point of departure, Vilanova Artigas initiated the so-called Paulista school of architecture in the early 1950s, involving such figures as Paulo Mendes da Rocha, Rino Levi and Lina Bo Bardi. Around the same time the Brazilian poet Ferreira Gullar published his Neoconcrete Manifesto, which sought to further an already fertile exchange between European and Latin American concrete artists. This movement led to the emergence of such distinguished artists as Mary Vieira, Lygia Clark and the ubiquitous Athos Bulcão. All of this seems to have been accompanied by a pivotally progressive movement on a global scale, when the neocolonial strategy of the Pax Americana was more moderate and when the detente of the Cold War served, however inadvertently, to sustain a balance between the postwar neocapitalist welfare state and the so-called communist bloc; a moment when commodification on a global scale had yet to begin, when the rainforests were still relatively intact and the transformation of the climate had yet to attain its tipping point. That Brasilia was realized on the crest of such a promising

historical wave is movingly evoked through the elegiac photographs of the French photographer Marcel Gautherot taken between 1956 and 1960, during a time when the initial core of the new capital was under construction.

Born in 1910, of working-class origin, Gautherot had studied architecture and interior design at the École des Arts Decoratifs, Paris, before being encouraged in 1936 by the creation of the Musée de l'Homme to document the daily life of ordinary people who, throughout the world, were still part of a culturally rooted pre-industrial economy. It was this ethnographic impulse that first brought Gautherot to Brazil in 1939 to document the folk culture of the Amazon delta. Fifteen years later, he would approach his documentation of Brasilia *en chantier* in much of the same spirit. Gautherot's images of the hinterland capital under construction in the midst of an underpopulated high *cerrado* plain, re-surface today like the forgotten stills of a social realist film, in which the steel frame of the twenty-eight-storey Congress building rises like a mirage out of the swirling dust of the bulldozed savannah. As a committed socialist who had come to his maturity at the time of the French Popular Front, just prior to the tragic denouement of the Spanish Civil War, Gautherot seems to have regarded the construction of Brasilia as a seminal moment in the history of what was then the first multiracial modernizing state. Close to the spirit of such socially committed photographers as Henri Cartier-Bresson, Robert Capa and Tina Modotti, Gautherot seems to have seen this moment as a point of convergence between the enlightened visions of a Brazilian elite and the heroic energy of a nomadic peon underclass, the so-called *candangos*, who came to Brasilia in their thousands to build, in the space of three years, the government complex and the Ministerial Esplanade, working around the clock, twenty-four hours a day. In spite of the arduous, not to say dangerous, working conditions, these 'wretched of the earth'—to quote Frantz Fanon—seem nonetheless to have had an intimation that they were participating in an historical event of world-transforming status. One senses that, despite their hard lives, they would have endorsed the words of the poet Vinicius de Moraes, who for the inauguration of the capital in 1960 wrote his *Sinfonia da Alvorada* [literally 'symphony of the dawn'], carrying the evocative lines: 'Yes, he [Lucio Costa] would plant in the desert a very white and very pure city [...] a city of happy people.' At the same time, it is a sobering fact that Gautherot's images of the harsh lives of these workers, sequestered in their encampments and ad hoc temporary shelters made of building scrap, were not published during the first phase of Brasilia's construction, unlike the supposedly more objective record taken by the official photographer Mário Fontenelle.

Be this as it may, it is touching to discover that the first presidential residence—the two-storey, mono-pitched Catetinho 'palace', built entirely of wood in the middle of the bush in the space of ten days in 1956 to the designs of Oscar Niemeyer—was as rudimentary as the timber barracks constructed by Novacap [The New Capital Building Company] for the accommodation of the peon workforce. As a decidedly provisional equivalent of the traditional presidential residence in Rio de Janeiro, this diminutive 'palace'[1] testifies, as much as any other undertaking, to the longstanding friendship between Niemeyer and Juscelino Kubitschek. It is hard to imagine anything more intimate than this six-room, first-floor presidential suite accessed directly from a verandah overlooking the bush. The presence of a rudimentary bar within this belvedere leads one to imagine the presidential entourage arriving by Dakota on the nearby airstrip, in failing light.

None of the modern capital cities founded after the Second World War can quite equal Brasilia for the monumental, geomantic character of its conception and for the subsequent speed of its systematic realization. Patently influenced by Le Corbusier but transcending his 'radiant city' vision, Lucio Costa's Pilot Plan took the remote cultural legacy of the antique world as its fundamental point of departure—from the axial grandeur of Egypt to the cosmogonic foundational paradigms of the Roman Empire. Hence the *cardo* and the *decumanus* that informed Costa's initial sketch, the much-noted secular cruciform that constituted the skeleton of his plan, assuming the silhouette of a giant bird falling on the site like the sign of a cosmic destiny. While the triangular head of this mythical bird—the symbolic nexus of the Three Powers Square—was never realized according to its initial form, the north and south residential wings of its infrastructure were fully developed, in the first instance by the superquadra housing blocks that occupied the southern wing and, in the second, by the denser and more varied housing blocks that eventually fleshed out the northern wing.

1 The word 'Catetinho' is also a diminutive of the name for the former presidential palace in Rio de Janeiro, 'Palácio do Catete'.

Aerial view of the Catetinho, *c.* 1958
South wing superquadra, *c.* 1960

The Three Powers Square seen from the Planalto palace ramp; in the foreground, the Federal Supreme Courthouse; to the right, the Museu da Cidade, *c.* 1960

South wing superquadra, *c.* 1960

Superquadra

The concept of a neighbourhood unit, as we find this adumbrated in Clarence Perry's *The Neighborhood Unit* of 1929, has perhaps never been more deftly articulated and judiciously applied than in Brasilia's superquadras, conceived by Lucio Costa as an automotive residential settlement pattern, integral to his Pilot Plan of 1957. One may see his neighbourhood unit pattern made out of a cluster of four 'super-blocks', each measuring 985 by 985 feet (300 x 300 m), with housing slabs rising to seven storeys in height, as a fundamental re-working, not only of Le Corbusier's more sweeping urban vision of 1934 but also of the small-scale separation of pedestrian and vehicular traffic that characterizes the empiricism of Radburn, New Jersey, the canonical neighbourhood unit model of virtually the same date. The genius of this typological synthesis derives from the relative low density and also from the intermingling of cars and pedestrians freely moving in and out of the confines of each superquadra. Inspired by Le Corbusier's futuristic slogan that 'a city made for speed is a city made for success', Costa conceived of these superquadras as green enclaves fed by the measured movement of automobiles, circulating for the most part at grade. The normative perimeter of each super-block is marked out by a belt of trees rather than by buildings, the blocks being allocated in pairs, so to speak, to flank the commercial-cum-civic strips between them. These strips are equally accessible by foot from their adjoining super-blocks. A primary school was envisaged to be included within every set of four superquadras, while all super-blocks should have been complemented further by a kindergarten. Costa remained open to variations on this four-block

neighbourhood pattern with regard to the uses allocated to the communal interstitial strips. Typical of this last is the wide strip separating the superquadras south SQS 106 and 107, accommodating sports fields and a sizable cinema, while in others we find primary schools, churches, clubs or small shopping malls.

What is of equal consequence as a variant is the different disposition of the housing slabs within each superquadra, plus further permutations in terms of architecture, unit type and mode of access within each building. Thus where superquadra south 308 — known as SQS 308 — consists of nine slabs, orthogonally arranged while rotating in a loose spiral formation, within the confines of a landscape laid out by Roberto Burle Marx, the adjoining superquadra SQS 108, comprises eleven slabs, six of them being arranged in pairs, within the confines of the green belt enclosing the block. The super-blocks SQS 107 and 108, both designed by Niemeyer, employ a similar slab type in which vertical access is achieved via a free-standing elevator/stair tower, serving narrow external corridors shielded from exposure to the sun by thin, unglazed, perforated screen walls made of prefabricated concrete blocks.

The success of the superquadra system surely derives, in part, from the fact that all the housing slabs are elevated on pilotis which, while rhythmically articulating the space, permit visual and physical permeability beneath the buildings throughout the extent of each 985-foot (300 m) square. It is a characteristic of this type-form that — as in Le Corbusier's Pavillon Suisse of 1932 — all the slabs are built on podia upon which the pilotis take their bearing. Some of these podia double as concrete roofs covering underground parking. They moreover serve as generous thresholds from which to enter the building. Today, in certain instances, they have been re-faced in polished granite, imparting an aura that is unmistakably bourgeois. However, in the last analysis, the tranquillity and identity of the pattern largely stems from the limitation in height, permitting no more than six storeys above the pilotis. One cannot help wondering how Costa arrived at these criteria. Is it just a coincidence that the British architects Alison and Peter Smithson arrived at a similar conclusion when designing their Golden Housing project of 1952, namely that 'above the sixth floor one loses contact with the ground'? One of the more remarkable nuances of the superquadra pattern was the reduction of the height still further in the lower string of super-blocks in the outer east edge of the wings, where the housing units are invariably two or three floors in height rather than six, and the green enclaves are rectangular in plan rather than square. This string of blocks was added to the original plan, along with an outer ribbon of small single-storey houses, in order to provide low-income housing to the workers who built the city. A further modification was to increase the height from one to three storeys in the commercial strip of the northern wing in order to provide, in addition to the commerce, cheaper residential units above.

The fact that these last provisions proved to be inadequate is suggested by the asymmetrical development of Brasilia over the last half-century, leading to a distorted pattern of land use in relation to the symmetry of the original plan. Part of this displaced urban growth is due to the fact that the southern wing of the plan was developed in a manner that was more consistent as opposed to the pattern of occupation in the northern wing. This bias towards the south, following the momentum of the autoroute between Brasilia and Rio de Janeiro, effectively led to the spread of satellite cities that today effectively accommodate most of the population, housing some 90% of the three million people living and working in the region. In this regard, it is significant that the only fixed rail system of public transport operating in Brasilia to date is the subway linking the bus terminal in the centre of Costa's plan to the chain of satellite cities running out towards the south: Guará, Águas Claras, Taguatinga, Ceilândia and Samambaia. The presence of this metro link emphasizes the relative dearth of public transport in the city as a whole, despite the proliferation of regional bus lines. Given the wide autoroute running down the central axis, one wonders why there are no designated bus lanes, such as one finds in Curitiba. One also notes that, as of now, there are no plans to build high-speed rail connections between Brasilia and some of the closer state capitals, such as Goiânia or Belo Horizonte.

Access to south wing superquadras on the South-East parkway, *c.* 1960

Aerial view of early construction work on the Monumental Axis, *c.* 1958

Axis mundi

Without the decisive axis of Lucio Costa's Pilot Plan, Brasilia as the modern capital would hardly exist. It would just be one more late-modern megalopolis endlessly expanding in the middle of nowhere. Among other things, Costa was prescient enough to conceive of his auto-infrastructure as a multi-level parkway system, emulating but totally transcending the famous parkways built by Robert Moses around New York during the 1930s. Irrespective of whether it is a question of the north–south superquadra link or the east–west monumental spine focusing on the Congress and the Ministerial Esplanade, there is little doubt that Brasilia remains, even now, one of the most efficient automotive greenway cities anywhere in the world. This ample capacity partially explains the empty character of this 3,000-foot-wide (915 m) monumental parkway, extending for some seven miles (11 km) in length and layered on either side of its axis with successive tiers of medium-rise office blocks attached to the ministerial buildings by tunnels and overpasses to either side of the central esplanade.

These bureaucratic annexes exemplify that nemesis of modern urbanism, namely that 'the space of public appearance', in the antique sense of the term, tends to emerge today largely within the built form rather than in the ostensible public space of the city itself. Moreover, given our increasingly paranoid craving for security, this has regrettably become the case even with the elevated platform that carries the bowl of the Chamber of Representatives and the dome of the Senate. Thus, despite its ostensibly public character, this metaphysical agora in the very heart of the city is no longer publicly accessible. Perhaps nowhere has the De

Chiricoesque aura of this *res publica* been better represented than in Gautherot's photographs, dating from 1962, in which sundry persons are depicted standing on this datum like characters from an Antonioni film.

This could hardly be in greater contrast to the Ministry of Foreign Affairs, the so-called Palácio do Itamaraty, which, to one side of the main axis, is ultimately the most representative public space within the entire civic complex, in terms of symbolizing the prestige of the nation state, in contrast to the indifferently furnished and convoluted system of public access to the two chambers of the National Congress. In the Itamaraty, everything turns on the minimalist syntax of Niemeyer's theatrical imagination. Here, the first floor already establishes itself as a total work of art in as much as its clear span of 100 feet (30 m) between one wall and the next is focused upon three artworks, Mary Vieira's aluminium sculpture, Roberto Burle Marx's garden and Athos Bulcão's trellis, not to mention Niemeyer's spiral staircase which, with its cantilevered concrete steps, leaps like a free form in space to the floor above. This upper floor is graced by an equally theatrical stairway, which conducts the visitor to the final floor, from which access is gained to one of the most spectacular views of the central axis. Here, as in most of Niemeyer's finest works, the viewer is confronted by monumental artworks of the highest quality, including two large paintings by Portinari and an enormous tapestry by Burle Marx covering the entirety of one wall. Herein a tropical roof garden, various antique furnishings and a series of historical vignettes present the visitor with traces of Brazilian history.

Niemeyer's latter-day Carioca manner — that is to say, his version of the New

Monumentality (c.f. Sigfried Giedion's 'Nine Points on Monumentality' of 1943) — dates from his preoccupation with the image of a levitating palazzo, which we seem to encounter repeatedly from the Alvorada palace onwards, notwithstanding the more substantial, arcuated form of the Itamaraty palace, the base of which may also be seen as equally atectonic by virtue of the way in which its foundations descend into a reflecting pool on all sides. Perhaps there is a correspondence here between the seeming emptiness of these formal gestures and the relatively undeveloped civic character of the institutions they represent.

Beyond the head of the Monumental Axis, the spirit of the hinterland (*sertão*) reasserts itself in the diffuse expanse that unfolds on either side between the Three Powers Square and the panoramic lake. It is as though, despite Costa's compliance with Sir William Holford's advice to bring the prow of the axis closer to the lake, it was somehow never possible to bring it close enough. The topographic consequence is that one has the feeling there would be nothing beyond the axis at all were it not for the Alvorada palace, still rather indecisively related to the lake, along with the somewhat random proliferation of embassies and the ill-defined campus plan of Brasilia's university. This last seems to have been inadvertently blocked by the barrier of Niemeyer's almost 2,625 foot long (800 m), introspective galleria-cum-faculty building — a brilliant, pre-emptive stroke that has so far prevented a more open-ended, orthogonal campus from coming into being. At the same time, the embassies, which of necessity vary greatly in terms of their representational presence and architectural quality, are so ill-related to one another that there seems to be little chance of their ever giving rise to an urbane diplomatic quarter.

The ever-burgeoning bush is everywhere on this peninsular, and here, as elsewhere, Brasilia suffers from too much space between one building and the next, so that — despite the promising monumental image of a new civilization — a generic public realm of a truly human scale and a correspondingly rich, institutional core have so far failed to emerge. One could say that, for all its heroic status as a national capital, Brasilia remains the unfinished modern project *par excellence*, suspended between the seemingly unplanned, postmodern, laissez-faire economy of its satellite cities and the planned but still far from consummated modernist vision of an entirely new way of life.

NORTH AUTOROUTE

MONUMENTAL AXIS

LAKE PARANOÁ

◄ 15

SOUTH AUTOROUTE

◄ 16

11 |

◾ 12

1   Bus terminal
2   National Theatre
3   Banco do Brasil headquarters
4   Brasilia Cathedral
5   Ministerial Esplanade
6   Itamaraty palace
7   National Congress palace
8   Three Powers Square
9   Planalto palace
10   Federal Supreme Courthouse
11   Brasilia Palace Hotel
12   Alvorada palace
13   Cine Brasilia
14   South wing first superquadras
15   Taguatinga
16   Núcleo Bandeirante

N

0   1km

III The Plates

Preceding pages:
Western view of the Ministerial Esplanade and the National Congress palace
under construction, c. 1958. All of the public buildings in Brasilia photographed
by Marcel Gautherot were designed by architect Oscar Niemeyer

Southern view of the Monumental Axis, with the Ministerial Esplanade
at centre and the National Congress palace to the right, c. 1958

Northern view of the Monumental Axis, with the Planalto and the National Congress palaces at left
and the Ministerial Esplanade at right, *c.* 1960

The Ministerial Esplanade under construction, *c.* 1958

'The ministries and autarchies were arranged along this esplanade (what the British would call a mall) — a vast expanse of lawn to be used by pedestrians, parades and processions. The ministries of Foreign Affairs and Justice occupied the lower corners, contiguous to the Congress building, which they framed, as it were, the military ministries completing an autonomous square, and the others arranged in sequence — all of them possessing private parking lots — the last of them being the Ministry of Education, which was adjacent to the cultural sector and treated in the manner of a park, a more appropriate environment for the museums, library, plenary, academies, institutes, and so forth.'

LUCIO COSTA, 'Relatório do Plano Piloto' [Report on the Pilot Plan], *Brasilia* magazine, year 2, n. 22, Oct. 1958, p. 14

The Ministerial Esplanade under construction, *c.* 1958

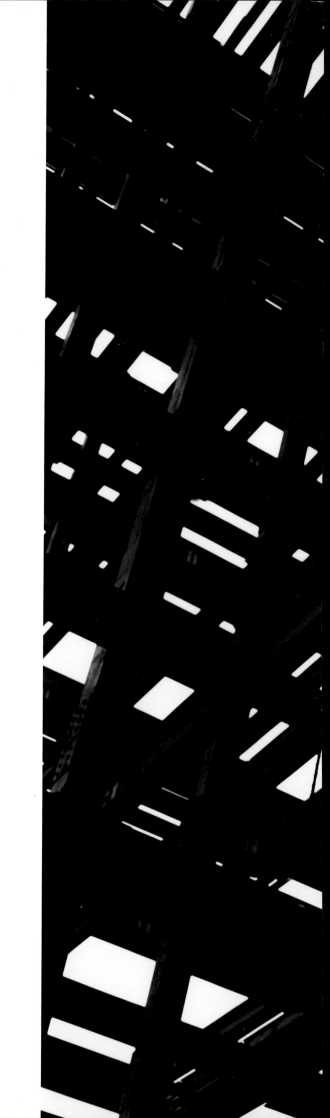

Detail of the metal structure of the ministerial buildings, *c*. 1958

Detail of the metal structure of the ministerial buildings, *c.* 1958

Ministerial buildings, *c.* 1958

The Ministerial Esplanade, with the National Congress palace in the background, c. 1958

The National Congress palace, *c.* 1958

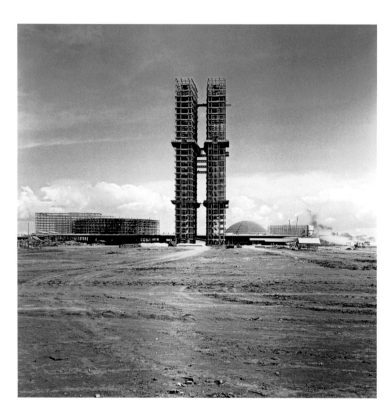

The National Congress palace, *c.* 1958

The National Congress palace, *c.* 1958

The Ministerial Esplanade, *c.* 1958

Labour Day demonstration in the Three Powers Square, *c.* 1959

Labourers on the Ministerial Esplanade, *c.* 1958

The Three Powers Square under construction, with the National Congress palace in the background, *c.* 1959

Labourer on the National Congress palace construction site, with the Federal Supreme Courthouse in the background, *c.* 1958 59

The National Congress palace under construction, *c.* 1958

Detail of the inverted dome structure of the Chamber of Representatives in an early stage of concrete consolidation, *c.* 1958

Early stage of concrete consolidation, Federal Senate dome, *c.* 1958

The Chamber of Representatives under construction, *c.* 1958

The National Congress palace under construction, *c.* 1958

The Federal Senate dome under construction, *c.* 1958

Concrete consolidation stage of the Chamber of Representatives dome, with ministerial buildings in the background, *c.* 1959

The National Congress palace, *c.* 1959

Labourers at work on the concrete consolidation stage of the National Congress palace, *c*. 1959

'In geographical terms, we are one of the largest countries on the planet, inhabited by a people who have been squeezed together. There are wide open grasslands throughout our vastness, a country yet to be conquered, filled with many admirable sites, and yet we gather in clusters by the sea shore, watching the tides roll in and out.

The founding of Brasilia is a political act, the consequences of which can be ignored by no one. It is the march toward the interior in its plenitude. It is the complete consummation of the possession of the land. We shall erect a powerful centre of radiation of life and progress in the heart of our country.'

JUSCELINO KUBITSCHEK, *Brasilia* magazine, year 1, n. 1, Jan. 1957

President Juscelino Kubitschek visiting a construction site in the new capital, *c.* 1959

Guerreiros [Warriors] sculpture, also known as *Os candangos* [The Labourers], by Bruno Giorgi, *c.* 1960

Guerreiros [Warriors] sculpture, also known as *Os candangos* [The Labourers], by Bruno Giorgi, *c.* 1960

In order to implement President Juscelino Kubitschek's decision to build the new capital in a thousand days, the Companhia Urbanizadora da Nova Capital (known as Novacap) was made responsible for the construction work which began in 1956 and was to provide services including housing, healthcare facilities and schools for the entire population.

Construction soon attracted thousands of workers from all over Brazil, especially from the northeast, who became known as *candangos*. The first census, taken in July 1957, recorded 4,600 men and 1,683 women, a population that leapt to 199,188 after the second census taken in September 1961.

Labourers, *c*. 1958

Portraits of labourers, *c.* 1960

Washerwomen on Lake Paranoá (under construction); in the background, the administrative towers
of the National Congress and the ministerial buildings, *c.* 1958

Labourers in the *cerrado*; in the background, the National Congress palace under construction, *c.* 1958

The Núcleo Bandeirante—then called the Cidade Livre [Free City]—was built late in 1956 to accommodate the first labourers who came to Brasilia, and consisted of provisional housing scheduled for demolition after the new capital's inauguration. It eventually became one of the first satellite cities, which were not supposed to have been established until the Pilot Plan's housing capacity had been exhausted.

At the same time, irregular settlements —the so-called 'invasions'—began to appear around construction site camps and other small urban centres of the period. One of these became known as Sacolândia (literally, 'bagland')—an allusion to the makeshift shacks improvised from cement-mix bags.

Núcleo Bandeirante, also known as Cidade Livre, *c.* 1958

Inhabitants of Sacolândia, on the outskirts of Brasilia, *c.* 1959

Inhabitants of Sacolândia, on the outskirts of Brasilia, *c.* 1959

Inhabitants of Sacolândia, on the outskirts of Brasilia, *c.* 1959

Makeshift dwellings in a camp on the banks of Lake Paranoá, *c.* 1958

Novacap workers on the Bernardo Sayão highway connecting Belém to Brasilia, *c.* 1959

Núcleo Bandeirante, also known as Cidade Livre, *c.* 1958

Novacap workers on the Bernardo Sayão highway connecting Belém to Brasilia, *c.* 1959
Workers, *c.* 1958

'For the Cathedral of Brasilia, architect
Oscar Niemeyer sought a compact solution
that would present itself externally with
the same purity from any angle. Hence
its circular form—a geometric, rational
and constructivist structure. Sixteen
pillars, contained within a circumference
of 70 metres [230 ft] in diameter, marked
the development of the façade, their
composition and rhythm symbolizing
ascension toward infinity.'

Brasilia magazine, year 2, n. 21, Sept. 1958, p. 14

Nossa Senhora Aparecida Metropolitan Cathedral (Brasilia Cathedral) under construction, *c.* 1960

Nossa Senhora Aparecida Metropolitan Cathedral, with the Ministerial Esplanade in the background, *c.* 1960

Interior of Nossa Senhora Aparecida Metropolitan Cathedral, *c*. 1970

Bronze sculptures representing the evangelists Matthew, Mark, Luke and John stood in the plaza in front of the cathedral building. Created in 1968 by Alfredo Ceschiatti and Dante Croce, the sculptures allude to the ones found in baroque churchyards, seeking to establish a dialogue between colonial and modern Brazilian architecture —not by chance the same relationship that may be observed in the architectural projects of Lucio Costa.

Os quatro evangelistas [The Four Evangelists] at the cathedral entrance, *c.* 1970

Palace of the Arcs (Itamaraty palace), *c.* 1970

O meteoro [The Meteor] sculpture by Bruno Giorgi, in the Palace of the Arcs (Itamaraty palace), *c.* 1970

Palace of the Arcs (Itamaraty palace), showing landscaping
by Roberto Burle Marx, *c*. 1970

Palace of the Arcs (Itamaraty palace), c. 1970

Aerial view of the Alvorada palace, *c.* 1958

Aerial view of the Alvorada palace, with Lake Paranoá already completed, *c.* 1958

'For Brasilia's residential palace, we sought to adopt those principles of simplicity and purity that characterized the great architectural constructions of the past. To this end, we avoided adding formally uneven or interrupted solutions or constructive components (such as marquees, balconies, protective elements, colours, materials, etc.) in favour of compact, simple choices through which beauty would spring from nothing more than proportion and structure.'

OSCAR NIEMEYER, *Módulo* magazine,
n. 7, Feb. 1957, p. 21

The Alvorada palace, *c.* 1962

Detail of the structure of inverted arcs at the Alvorada palace, *c.* 1962

The Alvorada palace, *c.* 1962

Reflecting pool in front of the Alvorada palace, with *As iaras* or *As banhistas* [The Bathers] sculpture by Alfredo Ceschiatti, *c.* 1962

Views of the Alvorada palace, with the chapel in the background, *c.* 1962

Reflecting pool in front of the Alvorada palace, highlighting the *As iaras* sculpture, c. 1962

Chapel at the Alvorada palace, *c.* 1962

'The National Congress encompasses all the services relating to the Chamber of Representatives and the Senate. Having both houses of Congress in a single building is an attempt to provide a more rational and economic solution to the problem, with no loss of the independence that is indispensable to them [...]

Architecturally, it must be characterized by its basic elements. In the case at hand, these elements are represented by the two chambers, for it is inside them that the country's most important problems are dealt with. We attempted to emphasize these in formal terms by situating them on a monumental esplanade, where their forms stand out as true symbols of the legislative branch. The blocks of the administration—the tallest in Brasilia—stand in the background, contrasting with the horizontal line of the esplanade [...]

The building looks out simultaneously onto the Three Powers Square and the Ministerial Esplanade.'

OSCAR NIEMEYER, *Brasilia* magazine, year 3, n. 25, Jan. 1959, p. 20

The National Congress palace, *c.* 1960

The National Congress palace, *c.* 1960

The National Congress palace, *c.* 1960

The National Congress palace, *c.* 1960

The National Congress palace, *c.* 1960

'For many years, Marcel Gautherot was our favourite photographer.

How many times did we travel together across Brazil! He photographed the buildings we designed. Pampulha, Brasilia, São Paulo... How well we got along and how easily we laughed with our dear old companion!

And the photographs he took... How well Marcel Gautherot was able to find the appropriate perspectives, the contrasts of the architecture he understood so well!'

OSCAR NIEMEYER, statement, 2000

The National Congress palace, *c.* 1960

The National Congress palace, *c.* 1960

O pombal [The Pigeon Loft] sculpture by Oscar Niemeyer in the Three Powers Square, *c*. 1962

'The buildings destined for use by the fundamental powers stand out from the complex. Three in number and autonomous, they are contained within an equilateral triangle, the appropriate elementary form drawn from the architecture of remotest antiquity. [...] There is one house in each angle of this public plaza—one might call it the Three Powers Square, with the Government and the Federal Supreme Courthouse making up the base and the Congress at the vertex, all three of them facing the wide esplanade arranged upon a second, higher, rectangular level.'

LUCIO COSTA, 'Relatório do Plano Piloto', *Brasilia* magazine, year 3, n. 25, Jan. 1959, p. 13

'The Federal Supreme Courthouse is the setting for the activities of the highest judiciary court in the land [...] The uniqueness of the project and the building's relatively modest proportions did not preclude the use of stately, noble features such as the ones appropriately underscored by the external columns and galleries.

The Planalto palace is the setting for presidential dispatches and includes all sectors directly subordinated to executive branch leadership.

In formal terms, the design is subordinated to the conveniences of unity that the Three Powers Square requires, striving to maintain the overall sense of purity and creativity that stands out in all of Brasilia's constructions.'

OSCAR NIEMEYER, *Brasilia* magazine, year 3, n. 25, Jan. 1959, p. 15

Aerial view of the Three Powers Square, *c.* 1960

Federal Supreme Courthouse, *c.* 1959

The Planalto palace seen from the Federal Supreme Courthouse, c. 1959

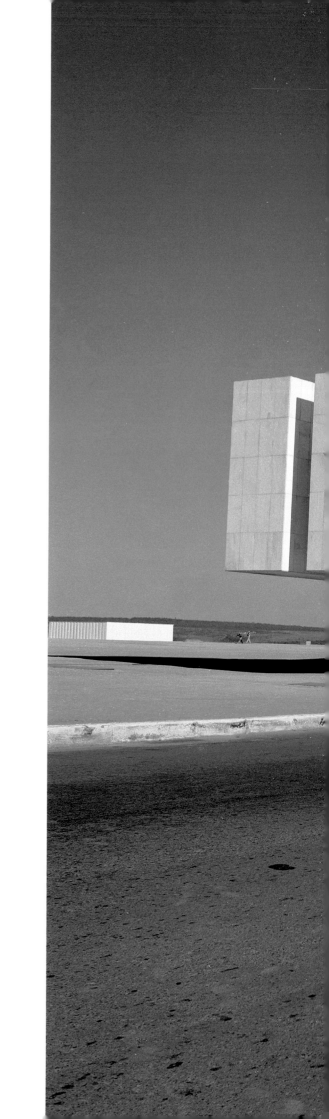

Brasilia's Historical Museum, with the Federal Supreme Courthouse in the background, *c.* 1960

The National Congress palace, c. 1960

Night and day views of Brasilia taken from the television tower, *c.* 1967

152

Cine Brasilia, *c.* 1962

Claudio Santoro National Theatre, *c.* 1967, located in the Northern Cultural sector, near the bus terminal.
The high-relief treatment of the theatre's exterior walls is by Athos Bulcão

Banco do Brasil building, designed by Ari Garcia Roza and Ivo de Azevedo, *c.* 1962

Aerial view of the bus terminal, *c.* 1960. At left, the Claudio Santoro National Theatre; at right, Brasilia Cathedral and, in the background, the Ministerial Esplanade and the Three Powers Square.

Bus terminal, *c.* 1960

Bus terminal, *c.* 1960

The Federal Supreme Courthouse seen from within the Planalto palace, *c.* 1961

Brasilia Palace Hotel, *c.* 1958

Brasilia Palace Hotel, c. 1958

Aerial view of the autoroute axis, *c.* 1960

Residential buildings designed for the Retirement and Pensions Institutes
that make up the earliest core of south wing superquadras, *c.* 1960

Residential buildings designed for the Retirement and Pensions Institutes
that make up the earliest core of south wing superquadras, *c.* 1960

The Monumental Axis viewed from Lake Paranoá (northern lake), *c.* 1960

Lake Paranoá (southern lake), with the Ministerial Esplanade in the background at left and the Alvorada palace at right, c. 1967

View of the Ministerial Esplanade and the Three Powers Square from the Avenida das Nações, *c.* 1960

View of the city as seen from Paranoá Lake (southern lake), *c.* 1960

Marcel Gautherot in Congonhas do Campo, Minas Gerais, with Aleijadinho's *Os Doze Profetas*
[Twelve Prophets] sculptures, *c.* 1942-1944 (photographer unknown)

IV Biographical Note

Samuel Titan, Jr.

Marcel André Félix Gautherot was born in Paris on 14 July 1910. Son of the mason Albert Félix Gautherot and the textile factory worker Alfrédine Apoline Meunier, young Gautherot apprenticed himself to an architectural studio while still at primary school and, in 1925, at the age of fifteen, he attended night classes in architecture and decoration at the École Nationale des Arts Décoratifs. He spent the following year in Strasbourg, working in a furniture store, but he returned to Paris and architecture school in 1927.

Gautherot continued his night studies in architecture until 1931, when he was inducted into compulsory military service. During those formative years (the latter half of the 1920s), he was influenced by the rise of modernist architecture, and especially by the work of Le Corbusier in France and by Bauhaus in Germany. In 1927, he visited the Weissenhof Siedlung, an estate containing twenty-one working-class dwellings built on the occasion of the 1927 Deutscher Werkbund exhibition in Stuttgart, under the supervision of Ludwig Mies van der Rohe with the collaboration of architects such as Le Corbusier, Walter Gropius and Hans Scharoun. In 1929, with fellow students, he entered a contest sponsored by the Austrian furniture company Thonet-Mundus: the group received two first prizes and two second prizes from a jury including Gropius, Van der Rohe, Marcel Breuer and Pierre Jeanneret. In 1930, Gautherot attended a congress of liberal, communist and socialist students in Sohlberg, Germany, where he delivered a lecture titled

'Discours sur l'architecture française' that was soon published by the socialist review *Notre Temps*.

After his year of military service in a barracks in Casablanca, Gautherot abandoned his architecture studies, as much a result of the need to seek employment as a consequence of his interest in photography. During the early 1930s, he joined Alliance Photo, one of the earliest important French photo agencies and, in around 1934, he made a photographic tour of Greece. At the same time, he participated in the cultural and political life of the French capital; his friendship with the photographer Pierre Verger and the poet Jacques Prévert dates back to these years.

In 1936, Gautherot began to work for the Musée de l'Homme, in Paris, where his tasks were variously expographic, architectural (he designed the museum's screening room with Robert Pontabry) and photographic in nature: alongside Verger, Gautherot shot pictures for the museum's ethnographic collections. That same year, the museum sent him to Mexico to photograph pre-Columbian cultural monuments and collaborate with the National Museum of Anthropology in Mexico City. Thus, Gautherot began to fulfill his longstanding dreams of travel. In Mexico, he visited locations in which Eisenstein shot parts of *Que Viva México!* and made the acquaintance of Manuel Álvarez Bravo, one of his 'model photographers'.

Back in Paris at the Musée de l'Homme in 1937, Gautherot still longed to travel. In 1938, he read Jorge Amado's novel *Jubiabá*

in a recently published French translation and began to make plans to visit Brazil. His prepared itinerary would lead him from the northeast to the Amazon and, from there, up river to the Peruvian Andes in order to see the remains of the Inca empire, after which he would return to Brazil to cap off his journey with Carnival in Rio de Janeiro.

Gautherot disembarked in Recife in May 1939, with a letter of introduction from the Musée de l'Homme and very little money to underwrite his travels. From Pernambuco, he moved on to the states of Pará and Amazonas, but his intention to go up the entire course of the Amazon River was soon thwarted by the outbreak of war in Europe. Called up by the French army, Gautherot was sent to Dakar, Senegal, but was demobilized shortly afterwards. With the occupation of France, Gautherot decided not to return to Paris. At the end of that year, he returned to Brazil, this time to Rio de Janeiro, to try his luck as a photographer.

In what was then the Brazilian capital, Gautherot quickly made friends and cultivated professional relationships with a remarkable group of writers and architects that included Alcides da Rocha Miranda, Carlos Drummond de Andrade (who dedicated a copy of his own *Fazendeiro do ar* [literally, Farmer of Air] to the 'fazendeiro da luz' ['farmer of light'), Lucio Costa and Rodrigo Melo Franco de Andrade, founding director of the Serviço do Patrimônio Histórico e Artístico Nacional (Sphan). This marked the beginning of a collaboration with the federal agency that lasted three decades. His first mission, which took place in 1940, was to assemble and photograph the pieces in the Lucio Costa-designed Museu das Missões. Gautherot travelled throughout Brazil at the service of the Sphan, and became a frequent visitor to the state of Minas Gerais, and especially to the historic cities of Ouro Preto and Congonhas do Campo, where he shot several photographic series of baroque architecture and the sculptures of Aleijadinho.

Through the Sphan group, Gautherot strengthened his ties with Rio de Janeiro's modernist architects and grew especially close to Roberto Burle Marx and Oscar Niemeyer. Gautherot developed a particularly warm and lifelong friendship with Burle Marx, while his affinities with Niemeyer were personal, aesthetic and political. Beginning with Belo Horizonte's Pampulha complex, by the mid-1970s Gautherot had photographed all of his friend's most important Brazilian projects.

To these patrimonial and architectural aspects, Gautherot was not long in adding a third focus of interest: Brazilian popular culture (or, in his terms, 'classic folklore'). During the 1950s, he became a frequent collaborator with the Campanha de Defesa do Folclore Nacional, directed by Edison Carneiro. Propelled as much by ethnographic interest as by political and personal sympathies ('I was more interested in the people because I myself am a man of the people'), Gautherot expended considerable effort in documenting Brazilian folk festivals—especially those of the northeast—and produced particularly remarkable photo essays in the states of Alagoas, Bahia and Maranhão.

Those first two decades in Brazil, during which Gautherot established himself professionally as a photographer, were also years of bohemian instability. Without ever holding down steady employment or earning a regular salary, Gautherot lived

in the artists' boarding-houses, cheap hotels and modest apartments of Rio's south zone while enjoying the friendship of Carybé, Newton Freitas, Lídia Besouchet and Manuel Bandeira, among others, and travelling around the country as often as he could. Even under such conditions, he never consented to a then-common practice among Brazilian photographers: he rarely sold negatives of his photos to clients, either public or private, and he kept a fairly comprehensive archive of his own work.

In the late 1950s, Niemeyer invited Gautherot to document the construction of Brasilia. For five years, which surely represent the apex of his career as a photographer of architecture, Gautherot recorded nearly every stage of work on the new capital. His images appeared regularly in the press, in architectural digests and especially in *Brasilia*, the official publication of Novacap, the public company responsible for the construction work. After the inauguration of the city, Gautherot continued to work on the subject, whether on commission from the Brazilian federal government (which sponsored a promotional series of international exhibitions) or in order to finish shooting post-1960 Niemeyer projects, such as the Ministry of Foreign Affairs and the Metropolitan Cathedral.

In 1961, Gautherot married Janine Monique Mille, an employee of the French embassy in Rio de Janeiro. They moved into an apartment in Rio's Santa Teresa quarter and, later on, to one in Botafogo. The couple had one son, Olivier, who was born in Rio de Janeiro in 1966.

In addition to the pursuit of his previous subjects, throughout the 1960s and 1970s Gautherot dedicated himself to photographing the work of Burle Marx, whom he accompanied on botanical expeditions and in whose architecture

office, in the Laranjeiras quarter, Gautherot established his photo lab, from 1965 until the end of his life. The extensive documentation of Burle Marx and Affonso Eduardo Reidy's Flamengo Landfill project, as executed under the direction of Lota de Macedo Soares, and Gautherot's photographs of his friend Jacques van de Beuque's folk art collection (the seed of Rio de Janeiro's future Museu do Pontal) are both noteworthy series dating from this period.

In 1986, Gautherot began to dedicate himself exclusively to organizing his photographic archive and to an unfinished book project (*Da Amazônia ao trópico de Capricórnio* [From the Amazon to the Tropic of Capricorn]). That same year, the French government bestowed the Order of Arts and Letters upon him; the following year, the Iphan (the organ that succeeded the Sphan) awarded him the Rodrigo Melo Franco de Andrade commemorative medal. In 1995, Rio de Janeiro's Casa França-Brasil held the first exhibition solely dedicated to his work, and *Bahia: Rio São Francisco, Recôncavo e Salvador*, edited by Lélia Coelho Frota, apeared on this occasion—the only book of Gautherot's work to have been published in his lifetime.

Marcel Gautherot died in Rio de Janeiro on 8 October 1996.

In February 1999, the Instituto Moreira Salles incorporated the Marcel Gautherot collection, comprising an estimated 25,000 photographs. In 2001, the IMS organized a retrospective exhibition of Gautherot's work and published a catalogue titled *O Brasil de Marcel Gautherot*. In 2007, the Fundação Armando Álvares Penteado did the same with the exhibition and catalogue *O olho fotográfico: Marcel Gautherot e seu tempo*, curated by Heliana Angotti-Salgueiro. Finally, in 2009, the IMS published two more books dedicated to the artist's work: *Paisagem moral* and *Norte*.

Marcel Gautherot photographing Mitla palace, Oaxaca, Mexico, 1937 (photographer unknown)
Marcel Gautherot in Bom Jesus da Lapa, Bahia, 1946 (photographer Pierre Verger)
Marcel Gautherot on Marajó Island, Pará, c. 1970 (photographer unknown)

Nossa Senhora Aparecida Metropolitan Cathedral under construction, *c.* 1959

V Chronology

Maria Beatriz C. Cappello

Sixteenth Century
In 1549, the city of São Salvador, in the Bahia de Todos os Santos, is founded by Tomé de Sousa as the seat of Portuguese colonial administration in Brazil. It is regarded as the country's first capital.

Eighteenth Century
Founded in 1565, the city of Rio de Janeiro becomes the seat of the colony's unified goverment in 1763; the captain general of Rio de Janeiro holds the title of viceroy. The earliest idea of moving Brazil's capital into the *sertão* is attributed to the Marquis of Pombal (1699-1782), secretary of the Portuguese state from 1750 to 1777. The Portuguese minister hoped to erect a new city in the country's hinterlands, intended to be the seat of government not only for the colony but for the Portuguese kingdom itself. Shortly thereafter, the independence conspirators from Minas Gerais include transference of the capital to the country's interior as one of the objectives of their movement. Joaquim José da Silva Xavier, also know as Tiradentes [the Dentist] (1748-1792), chooses the city of São João del Rei, in Minas Gerais, to be capital of the future Republic.

1808
After Portugal is invaded by Napoleon's troops, the Portuguese court seeks asylum in Brazil and Rio de Janeiro becomes the seat of the Portuguese empire.

1821
On 9 October, politician Jose Bonifácio de Andrada e Silva (1763-1838) advises São Paulo's congressmen 'to build a central city in the interior of Brazil for settlement of the court or regency, at the approximate latitude of 15 degrees, upon a healthy, pleasant and fertile site irrigated by some navigable river'.

1822
With the court back in Lisbon, a Brazilian court congressman publishes an anonymous pamphlet titled 'Aditamento ao projeto de Constituição para ser aplicado ao Reino do Brasil' ['Addendum to the Projected Constitution for Application to the Kingdom of Brazil'], the first article of which states that the capital of the kingdom shall be founded in the centre of Brazil between the sources of the Paraguay and Amazon Rivers under the name of 'Brasilia'—marking the first time the apellation is used.

1823
Once independence has been proclaimed, José Bonifácio de Andrada e Silva presents his 'Memória sobre a necessidade e meios de edificar no interior do Brasil uma nova capital' ['Reminder of the Need and Means for Building a New Capital in the Interior of Brazil'] to the General Constituent and Legislative Assembly of the Empire of Brazil, proposing a move to the recently created judicial district of Paracatu do Príncipe, in what is currently the region of the Minas Gerais triangle. He suggests that the new city be called Petrópolis or Brasilia.

1839
Writing from Lisbon to the Brazilian Geographic Institute, historian Francisco Adolfo de Varnhagen, viscount of Porto Seguro, once more takes up the idea of moving into the hinterlands, coming out in favour of moving the seat of government first to São João del Rei (in the state of Minas Gerais), and then to Goiás. In his texts, the move towards the interior becomes a national cause, and Varnhagen returns to it in various writings, particularly in *A questão da capital: marítima ou no interior?* [The Question of the Capital: Maritime or Interior?] (1877).

1852-1853
In 1852, inspired by Varnhagen, Antônio Francisco de Paula de Holanda Cavalcanti de Albuquerque (1797-1863) introduces a Senate bill to deal with the first draft of a legislative bill to move the capital to the country's interior, on the Central Plateau, 'at 10 and 15 degrees south latitude'. The project was not discussed by the senators until the following year.

1883
On 30 August, Saint João Bosco—the sanctified Italian priest Dom Bosco (1815-1888)—has a 'dream vision' in which he foresees the appearance of a 'Promised Land of unconceivable riches' between the 15th and 20th parallels of south latitude, in Brazil. This corresponds precisely to the location of Brasilia.

1891
Following the proclamation of the Republic, in November 1889, the third article of the new Constitution (ratified on 24 February 1891) includes the decision

to move the capital to the Central Plateau inside a 5,560 square mile (14,400 km²) zone belonging to the Union.

1892-1896
Marshall Floriano Peixoto's administration (1891-1894) names the first exploratory commission Exploradora do Planalto Central do Brasil, led by engineer Luís Cruls (1848-1908), director of the National Observatory, whose mission it is to demarcate the area and undertake the necessary studies of the location. This commission (known as the Cruls Mission) demarcates the area foreseen by the Constitution in the state of Goiás—referred to from then on as the 'Cruls quadrilateral', and henceforth appearing on maps as a small coloured rectangle inscribed 'Future Federal District'.

1909
An early supporter of the generic principles behind the move into the hinterlands, writer Euclides da Cunha (1866-1909) describes 'the unfrequented places' of the Urubupungá, prophesying that that would be the ideal site for an 'extremely opulent [city] of the future'.

1922
On 18 January, President Epitácio Pessoa (1919-1922) signs a mandate establishing the area in which the new capital will be built and the laying of the cornerstone, to take place in the vicinity of Planaltina, in Goiás, on 7 September, in celebration of the Independence centennial.

1948-1955
On 4 August 1948, the Polli Coelho commission, appointed two years earlier by President Eurico Gaspar Dutra, presents a general report on the construction project which reiterates location within the same region studied and described by Cruls, while expanding the area to 29,730 square miles (77,000 km²). In 1953, President Getulio Vargas creates the Commission for Location of the New Capital in order to proceed with definitive studies regarding the site and precise area for the new capital. In 1954, Marshall José Pessoa Cavalcanti de Albuquerque (1885-1959) is appointed leader of the Commission for the Location of the New Capital and proposes the name of Vera Cruz for the city. In 1955, presidential candidate Juscelino Kubitschek (1902-1976) declares in Jataí, Goiás that, if elected, he would change the location of the country's capital.

1956
31 January marks Juscelino Kubitschek's inauguration as President of the Republic. On 4 February, he meets with Marshall José Pessoa Cavalcanti de Albuquerque at the Catete palace in Rio de Janeiro and, on 15 March, in his first 'Message to Congress', he refers to construction of the capital. On 18 April, the president sends Congress the 'Anápolis Message', along with a draft for legislation that proposes the name of 'Brasilia' and the creation of the Companhia Urbanizadora da Nova Capital do Brasil (Novacap), the company charged with the city's construction. The project is unanimously approved by Chamber and Senate alike. In September, after a visit from Kubitschek at his home in Rio de Janeiro's Gávea district, architect Oscar Niemeyer begins to draw up plans for Brasilia. On 19 September, the Pilot Plan Contest is launched.

The legislation that had been drafted in April becomes Law Number 2,874 on 19 September 1956. Its last article names the city: 'Brasilia'. The National Congress decides that the date for transferring the Republic's capital from Rio de Janeiro to Brasilia shall be 21 April 1960, to honour the anniversary of the death of Tiradentes, leader of the Minas Gerais conspirators. Architect Oscar Niemeyer is named chief of Novacap's Department of Architecture and Urban Planning. On 2 October, President Juscelino Kubitschek boards a Brazilian Air Force DC-3 at Santos Dumont airport and—for the first time—flies to the central plateau that is destined to become Brasilia. That same month, construction begins on the Anápolis–Brasilia highway. In October, construction work begins on the temporary (and Niemeyer-designed) Tábuas palace ['wooden boards palace'], known as the Catetinho, the first presidential residence in the new capital, financed by the president's friends. It is the first building to be completed in Brasilia, erected in less than ten days (from 22 to 31 October) by forty construction workers labouring day and night. It is inaugurated in November 1956, when Juscelino Kubitschek promulgates the earliest legislation pertaining to construction of the future capital.

Building of the Núcleo Bandeirante begins: it is destined to house labourers employed in the construction of Brasilia. Known as the Cidade Livre [Free City], it is meant to be temporary and eventually demolished after the capital is inaugurated.

1957
A henceforth monthly publication of the Novacap group, the first issue of *Brasilia* magazine is launched in January.

As members of the Judging Committee in the contest for the new capital's Pilot Plan, urban planners William Holford, Stamo Papadaki and André Sive visit Brasilia in March. 11 March is the deadline for submission of proposals: over sixty Brazilian architects and urban planners apply. On 12 March, the contest's judging committee is installed. It includes Holford, from the University College of London; Stamo Papadaki, a professor of architecture and urban planning from the United States; André Sive, a professor of urban planning in Paris linked to Le Corbusier's group; the engineer Hildebrando Horta Barbosa, representing the Engineering Club; architect Paulo Antunes Ribeiro, representing the Instituto dos Arquitetos do Brasil; and Oscar Niemeyer, the head of Novacap's Department of Architecture and Urban Planning. Assessment of the projects submitted takes place from 12 to 16 March.

On 16 March, the jury announces results: the first prize is awarded to Lucio Costa's project; the second, to the project by Borunch Milmann, João Henrique Rocha and Ney Fontes Gonçalves; the third is shared by Rino Levi, Roberto Cerqueira César and L. R. Carvalho Franco's project and that of M.M.M. Roberto; the fifth prize goes to the project by Carlos Cascaldi, João Vilanova Artigas, Mário Wagner Vieira and Paulo de Camargo e Almeida, that of Henrique E. Mindlin and Giancarlo Palanti and the Construtécnica S.A. Comercial e Construtora.

Brasilia's first wedding is held on 17 March between Mr José Vitório da Silva, a Novacap employee, and Miss Generina Maria dos Santos. The wedding is officiated by Father Oswaldo Sergio Lobo, the vicar of Planaltina.

In April, President Juscelino Kubitschek and architect and urban planner Lucio Costa visit the area in which the new capital is being built and identify the location where the Monumental Axis will be established.

In July, North American construction companies are hired to erect two ministerial buildings a month and to begin construction on the Paranoá River hydroelectric dam. That same month, the filling and levelling of the future Three Powers Square begins — the future site of the presidential Planalto palace, the National Congress and the Federal Supreme Courthouse.

The first statistical survey of Brasilia's population is carried out on 20 July: the city is inhabited by 4,600 men and 1,683 women.

September marks the beginning of construction work on the National Congress, the moving, filling in and levelling of earth for the Brasilia–Belo Horizonte highway and the so-called superquadra (or 'super-block') residential areas. The following month, Minister of Education Clovis Salgado inaugurates Brasilia's first primary school, built and maintained by Novacap, and designed by Oscar Niemeyer. That same month, the Ministry of Foreign Affairs opens a series of exhibitions about the future capital in Berlin, Bern, Vienna and Milan.

In December, architect Ludwig Mies van der Rohe visits Lucio Costa at the Novacap offices installed in the Ministry of Education and Culture in Rio de Janeiro.

1958

Construction work on the National Congress begins in January. Brasilia's first hydroelectric plant, the Rádio Nacional de Brasilia, regular telegraph service to Rio and the airport landing field's lighting are inaugurated in May, the latter making night flight operations possible in the new capital.

Urban occupation of the future Taguatinga begins in June. It is the first of the satellite cities. That same month, construction begins on the Planalto palace and the Federal Supreme Courthouse. On 18 June, construction work begins on the Ministerial Esplanade's metal structures. The Alvorada palace is inaugurated on 30 June to serve as a residence for Brazilian chiefs of state.

In July, American architect Richard J. Neutra visits Brasilia and lavishes praise upon the work of Lucio Costa and Oscar Niemeyer. The following month, Niemeyer moves to Brasilia in order to supervise ongoing construction work.

1959

The 1,370-mile (2,200 km) highway that links Belém to Brasilia is inaugurated in Açailândia, in the middle of the Amazon jungle, on 1 February.

On 30 April, Cuban president Fidel Castro visits Brasilia. On 25 August, French Minister of Culture André Malraux lays the cornerstone for Brasilia's Maison de France. That same month — from a helicopter — film-maker Frank Capra shoots six hours of film of Brasilia's principal construction sites.

Construction of the Metropolitan Cathedral begins on 12 September.

An initiative of AICA's Brazilian delegation (led by art critic Mário Pedrosa), the Extraordinary International Congress of Art Critics is held in Brasilia, São Paulo and Rio de Janeiro from 17 to 25 September. With the synthesis of the arts as their main topic, art critics, historians, architects and urban planners from many countries gather to discuss the new city. Participants include Giulio Carlo Argan, Bruno Zevi, William Holford, Meyer Schapiro, Gillo Dorfles, André Chastel and Tomás Maldonado.

1960

In February, the United States embassy becomes the first construction on the Avenida das Nações, in the sector reserved for embassies. The cornerstone is laid during a visit by President Dwight D. Eisenhower.

On 17 April, Israel Pinheiro (the president of Novacap) is appointed mayor of Brasilia. The new capital's inaugural celebrations begin three days later, on 20 April.

20992 20993 20994 20995

20996 20997 20998 20999

21000 21001 21002 21003

Several views of construction work on Nossa Senhora Aparecida Metropolitan Cathedral
on a contact sheet in the Instituto Moreira Salles' Marcel Gautherot collection, *c.* 1960

On 20 April, President Juscelino Kubitschek goes to the Catetinho and, from there, to the Three Powers Square, where he receives the key to the city from the hands of Israel Pinheiro. At 11.45 p.m., on an altar built in the Palace of Justice, Cardinal Manoel Gonçalves Cerejeira begins the celebration of mass; at midnight, the bells of Ouro Preto (once the centre of the Minas conspiracy's historical independence movement) ring out to announce the historic moment at which Brasilia becomes the capital of the Republic of the United States of Brazil.

On 21 April, at precisely 9.30 a.m., the three governmental powers are established in Brasilia.

Finally, on 22 April, the Pilot Plan's first film theatre is inaugurated.

Also on this day, the following buildings are ready: the Alvorada palace and the presidential chapel; the Brasilia Palace Hotel; the Federal Supreme Courthouse; the Planalto palace; the National Congress; eleven ministerial buildings; the Escola Parque; eight double modules of stores and warehouses; military quarters for the 6th Company of Guards; the Central Telefônica Sul; the Ipê, Torto and Tamanduá model estates; the Department of Medical Assistance; the Zoo; the Escola-Classe; the Colégio Dom Bosco; offices for the Departments of Construction and Urban Planning and Architecture; the airport hangar; the Museu de Brasilia; the Paranoá Club; the Diretoria de Rotas Aéreas; Postal and Telegraph Services; the childcare centre; the Unidade de Vizinhança supermarket; a few residential blocks and some collective housing; offices and fourteen commercial establishments.

On 12 September, the bus terminal and the district hospital of Brasilia are inaugurated, and the cornerstone is laid for the new Itamaraty palace, future seat of the Ministry of Foreign Affairs. On 22 September, President Juscelino Kubitschek receives Jean-Paul Sartre and Simone de Beauvoir.

1961

Jânio da Silva Quadros is sworn in as president on 31 January. Brasilia celebrates its first anniversary on 21 April.

Law Number 3,998 (dated 15 December) creates the University of Brasilia, located in the north wing of the Pilot Plan, on the shores of the lake.

A new census is taken in September: Brasilia's population has grown to 199,188.

1970

Oscar Niemeyer's last two great projects for Brasilia are concluded. The Itamaraty palace is officially inaugurated on 20 April and Nossa Senhora Aparecida Metropolitan Cathedral (also known as the Brasilia Cathedral) — construction work on which had begun in September 1959 — is completed on 31 May.

1987

The urban complex of Brasilia's Pilot Plan is registered by Unesco as a World Heritage site of cultural and historical significance.

Residential buildings designed for the Retirement and Pensions Institutes
that make up the south wing's earliest core of superquadras, *c.* 1960

Acknowledgments
Adalberto Vilela
Ana Paula Hisayama
Andrey Schlee
Danilo Macedo
Eduardo Monezi
Eduardo Rossetti
Francisco Leitão
José Tavares Correia de Lira
Kenneth Frampton
Paulo Mendes da Rocha
Raniere Soares
Sylvia Ficher
Viviane Thomaz

Special acknowledgments
to the Instituto Moreira Salles
photography team
Cristina Zappa
Virgínia Albertini
Ailton Alexandre da Silva
Alexandre Piedade
Anne Greiber
Bruna Stamato dos Santos
Cídio Martins Neto
Daniel Arruda
Gabriella Vieira Moyle
Joanna Americano Castilho
João Gabriel Reis Lemos
Josiene Dias Cunha
Maria de Nazareth Bezerra Coury
Rachel de Rezende Miranda
Tatiana Ishihara
Tatiana Novás de Souza Carvalho

Portuguese text translated by Stephen Berg

First published in the United Kingdom
in 2010 by Thames & Hudson Ltd,
181A High Holborn,
London WC1V 7QX
www.thamesandhudson.com

First published in 2010 in hardcover
in the United States of America by
Thames & Hudson Inc.,
500 Fifth Avenue, New York, New York 10110
thamesandhudsonusa.com

British Library Cataloguing-in-Publication Data
A catalogue record for this book is available
from the British Library

Library of Congress Catalog Card Number
2010924961

ISBN: 978-0-500-51542-6

Printed and bound in Brazil

Inside jacket
Several views of the National Congress
palace on one of the contact sheets
in the Instituto Moreira Salles Marcel
Gautherot collection, *c.* 1960

Edited by
Sergio Burgi
Samuel Titan, Jr.

Editorial coordination
Cristina Fino
Samuel Titan, Jr.

Graphic design
Raul Loureiro
Claudia Warrak

Graphic production
Jorge Bastos
Acássia Correia

Map of Brasilia
Santiago d'Ávila

Research and captions
Bruna Stamato dos Santos
Cristina Fino
Gabriella Vieira Moyle
Maria Beatriz C. Cappello

Image digitalization
Joanna Americano Castilho
(coordination)
Daniel Arruda
Alexandre Piedade
Ailton Alexandre da Silva
Tatiana Novás de Souza Carvalho

Printing
Ipsis Gráfica e Editora, São Paulo, Brazil